Arts & Crafts Ideals

From The Book of the Roycrofters, *1900, A Roycroft motto showing the Roycroft Campus in winter*

Arts & Crafts Ideals

Wisdom from the Arts & Crafts Movement in America

GIBBS·SMITH
P
PUBLISHER

SALT LAKE CITY

compiled by
Bruce Smith, Yoshiko Yamamoto, & Gail Yngve

First Edition
03 02 01 00   4 3 2 1   D B

Copyright © 1999 by Bruce Smith, Yoshiko
Yamamoto, and Gail Yngve

Published by Gibbs Smith, Publisher
P.O. Box 667
Layton, UT 84041
Orders (1-800) 748-5439

Visit our Website at www.gibbs-smith.com

Edited by Gail Yngve
Designed by Bruce Smith and Yoshiko Yamamoto
at The Arts & Crafts Press
P.O. Box 5217
Berkeley, CA 94705

Printed and bound in the United States of America

Library of Congress Cataloging-in-Publication Data

Smith, Bruce. 1950-
    Arts & crafts ideals : wisdom from the arts &
    crafts movement in America / Bruce Smith,
    Yoshiko Yamamoto, and Gail Yngve.
        p.   cm.
    Includes bibliographical references.
    ISBN 0-87905-931-1
    1. Arts and crafts movement–United States. 2.
Decorative arts--United States. I. Yamamoto,
Yoshiko. II. Yngve, Gail. III. Title. IV. Title: Arts
and crafts ideals.
NK1147.S63 1999   99-35340
745'.0973--cc21   CIP

This book is dedicated with deep respect to Gibbs Smith for his efforts
through the years to bring into the
world of print important works about
the Arts and Crafts movement.

Bruce Smith and Yoshiko Yamamoto,
lovers of history and historical writing,
write on the Arts & Crafts movement,
bungalows, craft, and food. Together
they have written *The Beautiful Necessity: Decorating with Arts & Crafts.*
Smith has also authored *Greene and
Greene: Masterworks.* They own the
Arts and Crafts Press in Berkeley, California, where they print by letterpress
and hand bind books and the periodi-
cal *The Tabby: A Chronicle of the Arts
and Crafts Movement.*

Gail Yngve, lover of books and writing, is an editor, professor, and Arts
and Crafts enthusiast. She received
an MFA in Creative Writing from
George Mason University in Fairfax,
Virginia, where she was the recipient
of the Dan Rudy Fiction Prize. Her articles, essays, and short stories have
appeared in a variety of literary and
student-related magazines. She now
lives in a charming bungalow in Utah.

CONTENTS

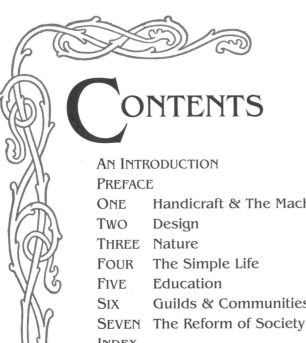

A quotation by John Ruskin that was printed as a motto in the 1900 catalogue The Book of the Roycrofters

Ruskin (1819–1900), an art historian who was the philosophical father of the Arts and Crafts movement in England, articulated the anti-industrial sentiments in his books, notably The Seven Lamps of Architecture *(1849) and* The Stones of Venice *(1851). He admired Gothic architecture and praised the medieval era for its integration of art and craft, individual and society. His writings were a major source of inspiration for the Arts and Crafts movement in America.*

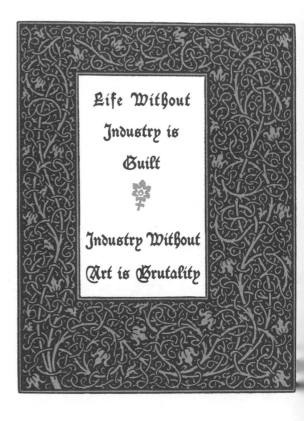

An Introduction

THERE IS A BURNING PASSION in the writings that define the Arts and Crafts movement in America. Far more than being concerned with mere style, the carefully written agendas encompass political, social, economic, and moral improvements as well as the reform of nineteenth-century design. From the origins of the movement in England through its transformation into something uniquely American, it evolved from a moral crusade against the evils of industrialization into a movement of dictates concerning ways of adapting and adjusting to a rapidly changing society. Writings in period books and magazines dealt with such issues as quality in craftsmanship, the meaning of art, the degenerating nature of factory labor, a redefining of education, the drive for community, the ultimate goodness of nature, and the sacredness of home. Though never organized systematically under one doctrine, the movement nonetheless held a powerful appeal to those who felt the need to reform, to improve the life around them, and fortunately attracted many men and women at the turn of the century whose progressive impulses could have been otherwise left disunited.

7

Arts and Crafts Ideals

ARTS & CRAFTS IDEALS is a collection of these writings drawn from a broad range of turn-of-the-century American writers who felt the need to give voice to their perspectives on the Arts and Crafts movement in America. It is natural that those who raised their voices the loudest are those most remembered today. Gustav Stickley, the manufacturer of Craftsman furniture who turned publisher, and Elbert Hubbard, the publisher of the magazine *The Philistine* who turned to manufacturing crafts, are today the two most often cited for their writings. But beginning in 1891 with the Boston-published *Knight Errant*, there were numerous other small periodicals devoted to the ideals of the movement, and even the major magazines of the day gathered from the Arts and Crafts movement in their defining of what was both fashionable and important. They included writings by regional architects on building, by craftspeople about materials, by educators advocating manual training, by intellectuals addressing economic reform, by social reformers on the improvement of daily life, and even by consumers on their hopes and disappointments toward the movement.

Preface

ATERIAL HAS BEEN CHOSEN for inclusion in *Arts and Crafts Ideals* in an attempt to represent both the range and depth of what was published around the turn of the century as well as the varieties of presentation: from essays to school prospectuses, poetry to household advice, and lectures to advertisements. It is by presenting this material that the authors hope the wide-ranging impact of the movement at that time can be realized. And indeed, on reading, sorting and narrowing the wide body of material available for inclusion, it must be said that the authors were constantly amazed at the material's direct applicability for today's world. But then, it is not a dissimilar time that we are passing through now. With the rapid changes happening around us, we face similar problems of finding meaning in our work, relevance in our art, and satisfaction in our home lives. In this light, we hope that the reader will find in these words we have chosen not just history, but more a way to see today's world; not just period advisements, but more a way to take direct action today; and, mostly, not just dated words of inspiration, but more pieces of writing that, even today, can give hope for our future.

B.R.S., Y.Y., & G.Y.

Chapter One

Ernest Batchelder, "Arts and Crafts Movement in America: Work or Play?" The Craftsman, *August 1909*

Batchelder (1875–1957) was one of the noted designers and teachers of the Arts & Crafts movement and operated the Batchelder Tile Company in Southern California between 1909 and 1932. He wrote magazine articles and the books Principles of Design *(1904) and* Design in Theory and Practice *(1910).*

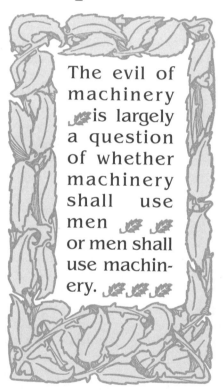

The evil of machinery is largely a question of whether machinery shall use men or men shall use machinery.

Handicraft & The Machine

A GREAT PART AND THE BEST PART OF A DESIGN MUST BE BROUGHT FORTH IN THE MAKING. One cannot design wrought iron, or carving, or furniture, or pottery, or any other object, upon paper alone, but on the anvil, with the gouge and mallet or the wheel, for these things, to have the true touch of the artist's self that makes the work worth the making or the having, must be wrought, not merely designed. The machine that is still a tool in no wise hampers the expression of the workman in his work, and is altogether good, but the product of such tools cannot be classed with machine-made things, and such tools help and do not hinder the individuality of a man's work, and through that his growth.

William L. Price "Art and the Machine," House and Garden, *October 1903*

ROSE VALLEY

Price (1861–1916), an architect, was also a founder of Rose Valley, an Arts & Crafts utopian community in Pennsylvania. The community produced furniture, pottery, and, with Horace Traubel as editor, published a journal, The Artsman, *from 1903 to 1907.*

11

Arts and Crafts Ideals

Joy in Work

From an address at the Detroit Society of Arts and Crafts annual meeting in 1917 by its first president, George G. Booth

The Society (1906– present) like the many other societies around the country, held exhibits, operated a sales room, and organized lectures and events. Its members included William B. Stratton, architect, Mary Chase Perry, and Horace James Caulkins of Pewabic Pottery.

rt is not a thing apart, an ornament added to life. It is the outward expression of man's struggle towards the ideal. Whether it be in the humblest homes or in the mansions of the rich, whether it be in the least of our institutions or the greatest, always there is some aim to achieve, some ideal to attain. This upward striving is in the very nature of man, and his aspirations and hopes are the wings of his spirit. In whatever form it manifests itself— whether we build our lives and characters true and fine, or do our daily work and service in truth, or fashion with our hands some simple article of linen or wood, clay or silver, the spirit has its opportunities for expression. To beautify our lives, to beautify the plain things of daily use, this is the simplest beginning in the world of art; for in art the spirit of man finds the means for the tangible expression of his achievements and his joy in work well and truly done.

Handicraft & the Machine

I N THE DISCUSSION of any subject, it is worthwhile to make one's self reasonably clear as to the terms employed. To attack all machinery without question of its powers or the method of its use, would be absurd, and to discuss the relative advantages of the handmade and the machine-made article, without consideration of the effects on mankind, both of the article made and the method of making it, upon the use and the maker, would seems to me to be equally a mistake. . . .

Mankind & Machinery

T o dismiss all machines on the ground that their product has in the main been unsatisfactory, would be absurd, because all machines are not of the same type. There are two broad classes into which machines may be divided, as were the sheep from the goats in the parable. There is the machine that is automatic in its operation, and which, simple or complex, makes a fixed product not due to the thought or control of the operator; and there is the machine which, simple or complex, remains a tool to be guided by the thought and volition of the artisan who works, not it, but with it, expressing, not the thought of the designer either of the machine or of the fabric, but his own thought.

W e are not now discussing the comparative values of the various products of machine or tool, but the effect upon mankind of their use.

William L. Price, "Art and the Machine," House and Garden, *October 1903*

13

The Grueby Pottery

With the advent of machinery the intimate relation of the potter to his ware disappeared. Here it has been resumed. Instead of the mechanical formality which has so often been mistaken for precision, every surface and line of this ware evinces the appreciative touch of the artist's hand. As in the old wares, there are no two pieces that are exactly alike, for while the general form may be maintained, every detail is a matter of individual regard. . . . Both in conception and design, in glaze and color, each piece of the Grueby ware is individual and of unusual merit, and deserves to take a prominent place amongst the best known wares.

C. Howard Walker, Keramic Studio, March 1900

Founded by William Henry Grueby (1867–1925) Grueby Pottery (1894–1920) was one of the largest producers of pottery of the Arts and Crafts movement. Though famous for thick green matte glaze and organic forms, their large scale production limited the extent of individual creativity allowed in each process of the work.

The Art and Craft of the Machine

Let us now glance at wood. Elaborate machinery has been invented for no other purpose than to imitate the wood-carving of early handicraft patterns. Result? No good joinery. None saleable without some horrible glued-on botch-work meaning nothing, unless it means that 'Art and Craft' (by salesmanship) has fixed in the minds of the masses the elaborate hand-carved chair as ultimate ideal. . . . The beauty of wood lies in its qualities as wood, strange as this may seem. Why does it take so much imagination just to see that? Treatments that fail to bring out those qualities, foremost, are not plastic, therefore no longer appropriate. . . . The Machines used in woodwork will show that by unlimited power in cutting, shaping, smoothing, and by the tireless repeat, they have emancipated beauties of wood nature, making possible without waste, beautiful surface treatments and clean strong forms that veneers of Sheraton or Hepplewhite only hinted at with dire extravagance. . . . But the advantages of machines are wasted and we suffer from a riot of aesthetic murder and everywhere live with debased handicraft.

From a talk by Frank Lloyd Wright (1867-1959) given to the Chicago Society of Arts and Crafts in 1901. The single most influential architect of the period, Wright was also instrumental in founding the Chicago Society. Unlike others opposed to or hesitant of machinery, Wright praised it as capable of "carrying to fruition high ideals in art—higher than the world has yet seen!"

House Beautiful,
January 1901

The Rohlfs Furniture

Like the International Studio, American Home and Garden, *and* Ladies Home Journal, *the Chicago-based* House Beautiful *(1896–present) was at the center of the spreading of the Arts and Crafts movement in America. It featured many articles on exhibits of the Arts and Crafts, on Frank Lloyd Wright's early architecture, in addition to running numerous articles on bungalows.*

HE "making of stuffs at a thousand yards a minute does not make men happier or stronger," nor is it in any way conducive to the best results; but giving a material expression to ideas that have been conceived in accordance with certain universal laws, and working out that expression with all the care born of a proper appreciation of their value, can only produce a result that is beautiful and consequently a source of joy to artist and possessor. William Morris demonstrated this beyond question, and beneath the experiments of Kelmscott House lay greater truths than are likely to appear to the casual observer at this short perspective. Gradually the leaven is beginning to work, and occasionally one hears of a tiny workshop where some earnest artist is trying by the work of his own hands to preserve ideas that to him seem worthy.

Handicraft & the Machine

One such shop is to be found in Buffalo, New York. . . . There are lumber, benches, lathes, tools of all kinds, paints, drawings, photographs, and furniture at every stage of development, from the first vague conception, perhaps, if one could look into Mr. Rohlfs's mind, to the finished product. And here lies the difference between this shop, or one of its kind, and that of the artisan. There is that inexplicable, intangible something in the atmosphere of the place that proclaims the presence of the creative spirit. One feels that here there can be no drudgery, no ennui; that the endless and delightful possibilities of all this raw material are ever revealing themselves, and that the most painstaking application in working them out is Mr. Rohlfs's chiefest pleasure.

Charles Rohlfs (1853–1936) operated his Workshop in Buffalo, New York, between 1898 and 1928. Beyond being utilitarian, his ornately carved oak furniture embodied his philosophy: "My feeling was to treat my wood well, caress it perhaps, and that desire led to the idea that I must embellish it to evidence my profound regard for a beautiful thing in nature."

17

Chapter Two

From Keramic Studio

Question: Is there something radically wrong with me because I must confess that, while I like to make conventional designs, copying a unit of design over and over on the china gets to be tiresome drudgery very soon, and I would admire a design just as much if it were reproduced by a mechanical process as I do when I know of the hours of back-aching, eye-straining work it takes to do it by hand. No artist can possibly do a conventional design as perfectly as it can be printed, and it seems like a great deal of wasted labor. At least in naturalistic and semi-naturalistic work there is some chance for individuality and improvement in the style of work. Is this rank heresy?

A. B. H.

Begun in 1899 by Adelaide Alsop Robineau (1865–1929) and her husband, Keramic Studio *offered readers technical how-to information on pottery and china painting, reviews of recent exhibits, and news about Arts and Crafts societies and clubs. Immensely popular, it served as a forum for the exchange of design ideas and philosophies.*

Design

Answer: We enjoyed this letter, even if some of A. B. H.'s remarks are rank heresy, as she vaguely suspects them to be herself. There is in her mind a serious misunderstanding of what constitutes art work. She says that no artist can possibly do a conventional design as perfectly as it can be printed. The reverse is rather true. The individual touch of a real artist is something that no commercial work, no mechanical process will ever reproduce. But it is very true that poor hand work is inferior to good mechanical work, and one should not imagine that because a china decorator, after taking a few lessons from a noted teacher, opens a studio, she suddenly becomes an artist. She has a long way to go yet. And it will not help her to borrow mechanical processes from the factory, that alone will stamp her work as inartistic from the beginning, and she will be at that great disadvantage with the factory that she cannot compete in price.

Art is thoughtful and creative workmanship. There must be in a work of art skillful execution, but there must also be thought and originality. . . . And only in conventional work can be combined what constitutes art work, good workmanship, thought and originality. The few hours of back aching and eye straining suffered in repeating a unit (and this work is tedious sometimes) are soon forgotten in the satisfaction of creating something. The naturalistic painter may acquire great skill in painting, but he never creates, just copies nature, more or less faithfully, generally less.

— signed, The Editor.

19

On Fitness

BE PRACTICAL TO THE UTTER-MOST. MAKE YOUR PLAN FIT THE SMALLEST AS WELL as the greatest physical need. Sacrifice symmetry, style, precedent, anything to it, but don't forget that the soul must be fed as well as the body. Don't forget that the home is to be the cradle of the ideal of the next generation, and the new truth that is to make the practical possible. Don't forget that modern steam power was the child of the teakettle, born at the fireside, and that art is the mother of all unborn mysteries, for it is through her we grow.

Will Price, "The Value and Use of Simple Materials in House Building," from House and Garden, *October 1905*

On Form

THE PRIMARY AND DOMINAT-ING IDEA IN MY POTTERY HAS ALWAYS BEEN FORM and color. Form is suggested by the use the article is intended for. In designing a shape the chief thought is how it can be most simply expressed and at the same time fulfill all the requirements for which it is intended. Take, for instance, a water jug; however graceful the lines, it can lay no claim to artistic excellence unless it also serves utility and convenience. If these qualities are united, the shape, usually, takes care of itself.

William Percival Jervis, Crockery and Glass Journal, *December 1909. An English Potter, Jervis wrote about pottery and glazes. From 1904 to 1905 he stayed at Rose Valley, later operating the Jervis Pottery at Oyster Bay, New York.*

Design

On Ornament

ORNAMENT IS STUDIED AND sought from by architects seeking public favor, at the expense of the mass, breadth, proportion and plan.

Samuel Howe, "The Use of Ornament in the House," The Craftsman, *November 1902*

On Architecture

AN ARCHITECTURAL PLAN IS not primarily made for the glorification of the architect. Neither is it a matter of elaborating buildings senselessly as a tribute to the vanity of human nature. If this were all, modern democracy would not hesitate to eliminate such an art by the simple expedient of neglect.

Bernard Maybeck, 1917.

An architect truly representative of Northern California, Maybeck (1862–1957) studied at the Ecole des Beaux-Arts in the 1880s. Later he created buildings that integrated the grace of nature and the whimsy of human touch merging diverse materials freely.

21

COMPOSITION

Composition, building up of harmony, is the fundamental process in all the fine arts. I hold that art should be approached through composition rather than through imitative drawing. The many different acts and processes combined in a work of art may be attacked and mastered one by one, and thereby a power gained to handle them unconsciously when they must be used together. If a few elements can be united harmoni-

ously, a step has been taken toward further creation.

Only through the appreciation does the composer recognize a harmony. Hence the effort to find art structure resolves itself into a development of appreciation. This faculty is a common human possession but may remain inactive. A way must be found to lay hold upon it and cause it to grow. A natural method is that of exercises in progressive order, first building up very simple harmonies, then proceeding on to the highest forms

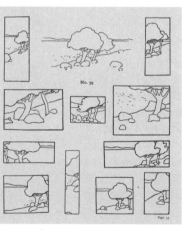

A page from Composition *by Dow*

22

Design

of composition. Such a method of study includes all kinds of drawing, design and painting. It offers a means of training for the creative artist, for the teacher or for one who studies art for the sake of culture.

This approach to art through Structure is absolutely opposed to the time-honored approach through Imitation. For a great while we have been teaching art through Imitation—of nature and the "historic styles"— leaving structure to take care of itself; gathering knowledge of facts but acquiring little power to use them. This is why so much modern painting is but picture wiring; only story telling, not art; and so much architecture and decoration only dead copies of conventional motives.

Good drawing results from trained judgment, not from the making of facsimiles or maps. Train the judgment, and ability to draw grows naturally. Schools that follow the imitative or academic way regard drawing as a preparation for design, whereas the very opposite is the logical order—design a preparation for drawing.

Arthur Wesley Dow, Composition, *1899. Dow (1857–1922), educator, painter, and woodblock artist, was a major influence upon the Arts and Crafts movement through his writings and his teaching at his summer school and during the years he taught at Columbia University in New York.*

23

The Simplicity of Good Design

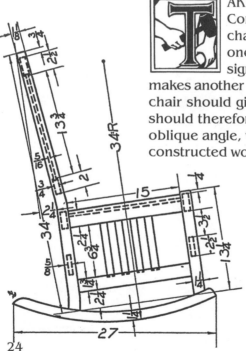

AKE FOR EXAMPLE A CHAIR. Consider first its purpose. All chairs are made to sit in. Yet one chair may be good in design for the very quality which makes another chair bad in design. The easy chair should give a chance to recline, and should therefore have the back at quite an oblique angle, while a dining-room chair so constructed would be obviously unfit for its function. The Morris chair, designed by William Morris, is an example of excellent design in reference to all these principles. The back is adjustable by a simple device, and the chair can thus be made to suit the comfort of the user to an unusual degree. The green cushions

Design

allow perfect cleanliness. It meets with equal success the other demands of good design. The material is suited to the purpose; the wood is without ornament, its beauty being brought out by the finish of the natural wood itself. The construction is so simple and straightforward that a child may understand it. Here "the problem of utility" is indeed "solved in terms of beauty." Fitness of form to function may be safely considered the most inclusive and fundamental of all the elements of good design.

May Dana Hicks & Walter S. Perry,
Prang Elementary Course in Art Education,
Sixth Year Book VII & VIII, *1899*

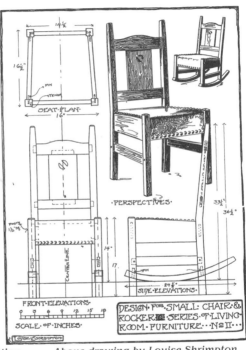

Above drawing by Louise Shrimpton,
a designer for Gustav Stickley

Chapter Three

Frank Lloyd Wright, The Cause of Architecture, *1908*

Architects of the Prairie School, such as Wright, designed long, low structures with broad horizontal bands of windows intending to reflect the quiet horizontality of the prairie. With clean, simple lines, they used details that echoed the natural fauna and flora of the region. One of them, George Washington Maher (1864–1926), explained how "each detail is designed to harmonize with the guiding motif, which in turn was inspired by the necessity of the situation and local color and conditions."

A Building should appear to grow easily from its site and be shaped to harmonize with its surroundings if nature is manifest there, and if not, try to make it as quiet, substantial, and organic as she would have done were the opportunity hers.

26

Nature

AMERICAN DEMOCRACY, in its myriad personalities, in factories, workshops, stores, offices—through the dense streets and houses of cities, and all the manifold sophisticated life—must either be fibered, vitalized, by regular contact with out-door light and air and growths, farm scenes, animals, fields, trees, birds, sun-warmth, and free skies, or it will morbidly dwindle and pale.

Walt Whitman,
Autobiographia, *1892*

A great spokesman of American romantic naturalism, Whitman's (1819–1892) poems expressed the yearning of men and women who were seeking to return to a life of greater simplicity, away from the materialism and false steps that civilization had taken. A generation later, his grand idealism provided inspiration for the practitioners of the Arts and Crafts movement.

27

FORM *follows* FUNCTION

LL THINGS IN NATURE HAVE a shape, that is to say, a form, an outward semblance, that tells us what they are, that distinguishes them from ourselves and from each other. Unfailingly in nature these shapes express the inner life, the native quality, of the animal, tree, bird, fish, that they present to us; they are so characteristic, so recognizable, that we say, simply, it is "natural," it should be so. Yet the moment we peer beneath this surface of things, the moment we look through the tranquil reflection of ourselves and the clouds above us, down into the clear, fluent, un-fathomable depths of nature, how startling is the silence of it, how amazing the flow of life, how absorbing the mystery! Unceasingly the essence of things is taking shape in the matter of things, and this unspeakable process we call birth and growth. Awhile the spirit and the matter fade away together, and it is this that we call decadence, death. These two happenings seem jointed and interdependent, blended into one like a bubble and its iridescence and they seem borne along upon a slowly moving air. This air is wonderful past all understanding.

Yet to the steadfast eyes of one standing upon the shore of things, looking chiefly and most lovingly upon that side on which the sun shines and that we feel joyously

Nature

to be life, the heart is ever gladdened by the beauty, the exquisite spontaneity, with which life seeks and takes on its forms in an accord perfectly responsive to its needs. It seems ever as though the life and the form were absolutely one and inseparable, so adequate is the sense of fulfillment. . . . It is the pervading law of all things organic and inorganic, of all things physical and metaphysical, of all things human and all things superhuman, of all true manifestations of the head, of the heart, of the soul, that the life is recognizable in its expression, that form ever follows function. This is the law.

Louis H. Sullivan, "The Tall Office Building Artistically Considered," Lippincott Magazine, *1896*

Sullivan (1856–1924), though best known for his commercial buildings, was truly the founder of the Prairie School of architecture and mentor to such as Frank Lloyd Wright, George Grant Elmslie, and George Washington Maher. He theorized that a form ought to be created from its inner core into functional and beautiful parts.

29

Elbert Hubbard, The Philosophy of Elbert Hubbard, *1930*

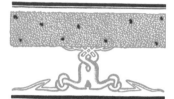

The ornaments and decorations on these two pages were designed by Dard Hunter (1883–1966) during the time he spent with Elbert Hubbard in East Aurora at the Roycroft Campus. A designer, papermaker, printer, and scholar, Hunter was at Roycroft from 1904 to 1910 except for a period of study in Vienna between 1908 and 1909. With a definite trace of Secessionist influence, his simple designs glorified many of the works of stained glass, furniture designs, and books that the Roycrofters produced.

GOOD HEALTH! Whenever you go out of doors, draw the chin in, carry the crown of your head high, and fill the lungs to the utmost; drink in sunshine; greet your friends with a smile, and put soul into every hand-clasp. Do not fear being misunderstood and never waste a minute thinking about your enemies. Try to fix firmly in your mind what you would like to do, and then without violence of direction you will move straight to the goal.

30

Nature

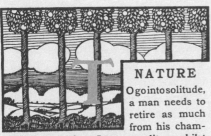

NATURE

To go into solitude, a man needs to retire as much from his chamber as from society. I am not solitary whilst I read and write, though nobody is with me. But if a man would be alone, let him look at the stars. The rays that come from those heavenly worlds, will separate between him and vulgar things. One might think the atmosphere was made transparent with this design, to give man, in the heavenly bodies, the perpetual presence of the sublime ❧ Seen in the streets of cities, how great they are! If the stars should appear one night in a thousand years, how would men believe and adore; and preserve for many generations the remembrance of the city of God which had been shown! But every night come out these preachers of beauty, and light the universe with their admonishing smile.

Nature, by Ralph Waldo Emerson, as printed by the Roycrofters with designs by Dard Hunter in 1905.

After leaving his ministry at the age of twenty-nine, Emerson (1801–1882) settled in Concord, Massachusetts, to lead a quiet life of writing, lecturing, and taking contemplative walks around Walden Pond, later made famous by Henry Thoreau. Emerson's paean to man's place in the world, Nature (1836), not only found great favor with Boston transcendentalists who were seeking lives of genteel simplicity, but continued to resonate in the minds of thinkers providing a spiritual core for the Arts and Crafts movement.

31

John Burroughs, "The Gospel of Nature," Century, 1912. Like other transcendentalists, Burroughs (1837–1936), a naturalist and romantic poet, stirred the imagination of men and women to go out and "share the great, sunny, joyous life of the earth."

William L. Price, "Choosing Simple Materials for the House," in Country Homes and Gardens of Moderate Cost, 1907

HOW THE contemplation of nature as a whole does take the conceit **Man's Place in Nature** out of us! How we dwindle to mere specks and our little lives to the span of a moment in the presence of the cosmic bodies and the interstellar spaces! How we hurry! How we husband our time. A year, a month, a day, an hour may mean so much to us. Behold the infinite leisure of nature.

THE ADVANTAGES of the use of common **Regionalism** and rough local materials seem to be threefold: First, they are cheap; second, they are easily obtainable; and third, they are beautiful. Burroughs says somewhere that a house should be built of materials picked up at hand, and in a large degree he seems to me to be right. Not only for sentimental and practical reasons but because it tends to produce types—tends toward a pleasing homogeneity in local style that is altogether good.

Nature

An Artistic House

THIS HOUSE GREW, AS ALL houses should grow, out of the needs of the owners and the opportunity offered by the site. In this particular case the site included an old stone barn, and as part of the demand was for two studios, the whole house may be said to have grown out of these facts. The barn doors fortunately opened north, and, changed to windows, gave the desired studio light; the pleasant outlook as fortunately lay to the south and included an old spring house that had crept in between the trunks of giant sycamores and nestled in the hollow so that its roof was nearly level with the ground. . . . The house rambles off from the fireplace and off the studios and is connected to them by an octagon stair hall. It is built in part of field stone so like that in the old barn that it is almost impossible to tell old work from new. The upper part is of a warm gray plaster, and the roof of red tile. All, the detail is as simple and direct as possible, and the interior is finished in cypress stained to soft browns and grays and guilty of no finish other than wax or oil. . . . It is what it was intended to be, the home and workshop of busy artist, and the grounds and garden growing up around it are of the simple and direct character that might be expected to result from the old environment and the new life growing up within it.

Ralph de Martin, "An Artist's House in Rose Valley," American Homes and Gardens, *March 1909*

Henry Mather Greene (1870–1954) with his older brother, Charles Sumner Greene, (1868–1957) formed an architectural partnership designing homes that were distinctively Southern Californian, yet imbued with the spirit of Japan. They designed furniture and furnishings as part of the house, each exquisite detail glorifying the beauty of the material and expressing the brothers' deep lifelong respect for fine craftsmanship.

THE IDEA WAS TO ELIMINATE EVERY THING UNNECESSARY, TO MAKE THE WHOLE AS DIRECT AND SIMPLE

AS POSSIBLE 🐝🐝 BUT ALWAYS WITH THE BEAUTIFUL IN MIND AS THE FIRST GOAL.... 🐝🐝

HENRY MATHER GREENE, 1912

Chapter Four

The Simple Life

An American Crusade

Under the editorship of Bok, The Ladies Home Journal *shunned the Victorian preoccupation with decoration and promoted to its very large middle-class female readership the virtues of Arts and Crafts simplicity. Bok published articles on "Good and Bad Designs" and the first series of model houses by such as Frank Lloyd Wright and Will Bradley. President Theodore Roosevelt wrote that Bok "changed, for the better, the architecture of an entire nation."*

THE AVERAGE AMERICAN WOMAN IS a perfect slave to the useless rubbish which she has in her rooms. . . . It is positively rare, but tremendously exhilarating, to find a woman, as one does now and then, who is courageous enough to furnish her home with an eye single to comfort and practical utility, and who refuses to have her home lowered to a plane of mediocrity by filling it with useless bric-a-brac and jimcracks, the only mission of which seems to be to offend the eye and accumulate dust. . . . The most artistic rooms are made not by what is in them, but by what has been left out of them. One can never quarrel with simplicity.

Edward Bok, "Is it Worth While?" The Ladies Home Journal, *November 1900*

The Simple Life

What One Needs

HOW LITTLE ONE NEEDS— actually needs—in this life where there is no competition, where there are no people. Outside, it is so easy to do without the little trifles of mundane life. Here, one change of raiment is enough and the wherewithal to wash and sleep. To be out in the open air, to be simple, to be at work, is happiness.

Jane Byrd McCall, diary, 14 December 1889

McCall (1861-1935), the wife of Ralph Radcliffe Whitehead, subscribed to the ideal of simplicity after her trip to Europe where she met John Ruskin and other Arts and Crafts practitioners. Taking her middlename for his new commune, Byrdcliffe, in 1901, Whitehead built an experimental arts colony in Woodstock, New York.

The Simple Life

MODERN MATERIALISM demands of far too many men an unworthy sacrifice. That the wife and children may live in ostentation the man must be a slave to business, rushing and jostling with the crowd in the scramble for wealth. A simpler standard of living will give him more time for art and culture, more time for his family, more time to live.

Charles Keeler, The Simple Home, *1904*

Keeler (1871–1937), a close friend of Bernard Maybeck, was a poet, naturalist, and civic leader who praised the virtues of the simple life. He warned readers of the dangers of modern materialism and extolled the simple home as the cradle of one's happiness, both materially and spiritually.

From Irving Gill's article "The Home of the Future" for The Craftsman

ANY DEVIATION FROM SIMPLICITY RESULTS IN A LOSS OF DIGNITY. Ornaments tend to cheapen rather than enrich, they acknowledge inefficiency and weakness. A house cluttered up by complex ornament means that the designer was aware that his work lacked purity of line and perfection of proportion, so he endeavored to cover its imperfection by adding on detail, hoping thus to distract the attention of the observer from the fundamental weakness of his design. If we omit everything useless from the structural point of view we will come to see the great beauty of straight lines, to see the charm that lies in perspective, the force in light and shade, the power in balanced masses, the fascination of color that plays upon a smooth wall left free to report the passing of a cloud or nearness of a flower, the furious rush of storms and the burning stillness of summer suns.

Irving Gill, "The Home of the Future," The Craftsman, *May 1916*

Gill (1870–1936) often worked in concrete and stucco to express the simple, geometric shapes and lines of the homes he designed in Southern California.

38

The Simple Life

HOUSES SIMPLY BUILT depend on natural projections and their shadows for ornament. 🍃

From a 1902 brochure by The Hillside Club, (1898–present). Formed in Berkeley, California, by poet and naturalist Charles Keeler with the support of architects such as Bernard Maybeck, Almeric Coxhead, and John Galen Howard, the club's object was "to protect the hills of Berkeley from unsightly grading and the building of unsuitable and disfiguring houses."

GRADUALLY THE DWELLER in the simple home will come to ponder upon the meaning of art . . . it will then become apparent how truly the home is the real art center. 🍃

From The Simple Home *by Charles Keeler. Written in 1904 during his presidency of the Hillside Club, this book eloquently proselytized newcomers to inhabit the Berkeley Hills according to the ideals set forth by the club. As he wrote, it was necessary to "emphasize the gospel of the simple life, to scatter broadcast the faith in simple beauty."*

The Keeler Home, Bernard Maybeck, 1894

Drawing by Mary Cardwell

Craftsman Simplicity

E HAVE PLANNED houses from the first that are based on the big fundamental principles of honesty, simplicity, and usefulness —the kind of houses that children will rejoice all their lives to remember as 'home,' and that give a sense of peace and comfort to the tired men who go back to them when the day's work is done. Because we believe that the healthiest and happiest life is that which maintains the closest relationship with out-of-doors, we have planned our houses with outdoor living rooms, dining rooms, and sleeping rooms and many windows to let in plenty of air and sunlight.

Gustav Stickley, Craftman Homes, *1909*

What Simplicity Means

O NOT THINK THAT simplicity means something like the side of a barn, but rather something with a graceful sense of beauty in its utility from which discord and all that is meaningless has been eliminated. Do not imagine that repose means taking it easy for the sake of rest, but rather taking it easily because perfectly adjusted in relation to the whole, in absolute poise, leaving nothing but a feeling of quiet satisfaction with its sense of completeness.

Frank Lloyd Wright, Architecture and Machine, *a speech given to the University Guild, Evanston, Illinois, in 1894*

The Simple Life

A Spirit of Simplicity

WE MUST SEARCH OUT, set free, restore to honor the true life, assign things to their proper places, and remember that the center of human progress is moral growth. What is a good lamp? It is not the most elaborate, the finest wrought that of the most precious metal. A good lamp is a lamp that gives good light.

What material things does a man need to live under the best conditions? A healthful diet, simple clothing, a sanitary dwelling-places, air and exercise. I am not going to enter into hygienic detail, compose menus, or discuss model tenements and dress reform. My aim is to point out a direction and tell what advantage would come to each of us from ordering his life in a spirit of simplicity.

CHARLES WAGNER

Charles Wagner, The Simple Life, *1901*

An Alsacian Protestant minister, Wagner internationally popularized the idea of simple living. Endorsed by President Theodore Roosevelt ("I preach your books to my countrymen."), Wagner lectured throughout the United States advocating the concept of "simple thoughts, simple words, simple needs, simple pleasures, simple beauty."

41

Chapter Five

School Arts

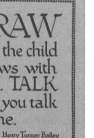

A ND THE TIME WILL COME when one generation can say as it contemplates the next:

I framed his tongue to music,
I armed his hand with skill,
I moulded his face to beauty,
And his heart the throne of Will.

Henry Turner Baily, "The Arts and Crafts in the Public Schools," An address before the American Institute of Instruction at New Haven, Connecticut, July 1906

Henry Turner Bailey (1866 –1931), a teacher and writer in the Boston area, devoted his life to the dissemination of applied arts from his own studio, Trustworth. For many years, he was the editor of The School Arts *magazine spreading the ideals of art and craft to children all over the United States.*

The School Arts Guild, from The School Arts *magazine, encouraged students to submit their work for a monthly competition.*

42

Education

Manual Training

What is needed in our public schools is a system of manual training which demands the employment of teachers who are masters in the craft that is taught. If these teachers are high priced, the country should pay the price, because no branch of education is more valuable than right training in this direction. . . . If a child has only a little time to devote to manual training, he should be taught only a little; but that should be as thoroughly taught as if he were to become a master cabinetmaker. He may not make many pieces of furniture, but what he does will be done well and the next generation will have better tastes and standards of work and art because of it.

Gustav Stickely, "Manual Training in the Public Schools," The Craftsman, April 1909

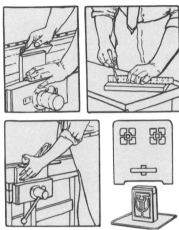

From as early as 1880 when the first manual training school was founded in St. Louis, educators sought to incorporate "hand and brain" in education through publications and by new curriculums in schools.

43

INTELLECTUAL education has run away with us. The balance necessary for a rounded-out culture can only be had when the practice of the arts as well as appreciation is a part of general community life. Machinery today has robbed us of the urge to be practical with our hands, but no machine has ever designed, and no design has been successful unless the material of its application was thoroughly understood by the designer. . . . With machinery doing the world's work there is time to spend in the daily life of all. Shall it be squandered, or will we really buy something with it? Pleasure

A Movement of Amateurs

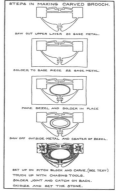

can be bought on the outside but happiness comes from within. The flare to create beauty is rare in a mechanical age, but within all humans is a smouldering desire, the divine heritage.

Emil Kronquist, Metalcraft and Jewelry, *1926*

Handcraft was not only for the professional artisan; it was advocated as being beneficial for those of the aspiring middle class as demonstrated by the popularity of such books as Kronquist's Metalcraft and Jewelry.

44

Education

MY FATHER TALKED to me from childhood about the importance of doing what I wanted to do, of being true to myself. He urged me to let my art rather than any financial consideration have first place in mind and heart as always. That was the finest lesson my father taught me. It has become my religion. 🌿🌿🌿

The Goals of Education

Bernard Maybeck, 1927

THE MAIN OBJECT IN EVERY SCHOOL should be, not to provide the children with means of earning a livelihood, but to show them how to live a happy and worthy life, inspired by ideals which exalt and dignify both labor and pleasure. 🌿

Charles Eliot Norton—quoted in Mrs. M. F. Johnson, "Arts and Crafts," Leaflet No. 10, Department Pamphlet No. 41, American Civic Association, Department of Arts and Crafts, 1906

Charles Eliot Norton (1827–1908), the first professor of art history in America, was a close friend of John Ruskin and was himself, in many ways, instrumental to the shaping and spreading of the Arts and Crafts ethos among the educated elite in America.

The Countryside as Education

THE REASON WHY I believe that the country is such a fine training-school for character and experience, is because farm work, as compared to the routine and the one-sidedness of office work, offers to a boy the best possible opportunities for the development of self-reliance, of initiative and of the creative faculty. . . . In the business life of our cities the city man who begins as a clerk rarely goes much further; he may be promoted to some higher position in the department in which he started but the career usually ends in the groove in which it began. Young people who enter routine occupations with no other experience back of them have no equipment for anything else, and they are apt to have little capacity for meeting new problems and forging ahead. Whereas the boy who has been brought up on an American farm and who has been trained in all the variety of experience that makes up farm life has acquired independence, ingenuity and the ability to think for himself. Every day on a farm brings some new

Education

problem that has to be met and solved. I have so often said, contact with Nature gives us a certain breadth of vision on which depends our capacity for further development. We cannot go forward beyond the limit of our vision. A mind crushed by the dull detail of routine labor and a physique depleted by unwholesome indoor occupation cannot lift a man out of the narrow sphere of drudgery. But a mind lit by the vision of a larger purpose in daily work and of something greater beyond that, a body vibrant with health and ready for action—these make a man, while loyal to his work, at the same time independent of it, because his thought and his capability are larger than the routine of his occupation.

Gustav Stickley, "The Value of a Country Education to Every Boy: A Talk with the Host of Craftsman Farms," The Craftsman, *January 1911*

Growing up a stone-mason's son, Gustav Stickley (1858–1942) took on the role of the chief spokesman and promoter of the Arts and Crafts movement in America. He made and sold his line of Craftsman furniture and furnishings, had mail-ordering of his Craftsman bungalow plans, operated an entire building devoted to his undertakings in New York City, as well as published a magazine devoted to the movement, The Craftsman. *In 1908, Stickley launched what was his most idealistic—and perhaps his most personal—project: the Craftsman Farms, to create a 650-acre craft and farming community in Morris Plains, New Jersey. He envisioned that the farms would integrate all the processes of work and shall "stand for the right of children to health and happiness, through an education that will develop hands as well as heads."*

A unique self-made man, Elbert Hubbard (1856–1915) became a champion of marketing the Arts and Crafts in America. He gathered talented craftspeople and local workers together at his Roycroft Campus in East Aurora, New York, producing books, periodicals, furniture, metalwork, leatherwork, lighting, china and stained glass. For his workers as well as visitors to Roycroft, he organized weekly lectures, concerts, and offered evening classes and piano lessons, believing that one's "health of mind and health of body" served to benefit society at large.

E ducation comes through doing things, making things, going without things, taking care of yourself, talking about things.

Elbert Hubbard, The Philosophy of Elbert Hubbard, *1930*

48

Education

Contentment dwells with common folks, who well their hours employ. Green fields about, blue sky above Gem sorrows & much joy.

For Children

HE various manifestations and examples of this influence (of the Arts and Crafts movement) may be noted as we may find them affecting the child; affecting the workers; and affecting the consumers. Much stress is laid today on the artistic environment of the child. In some of the beautiful nurseries and private homes hygienic science and the love of the beautiful have made paradises for some favored little mortals. We also happily find this shown in the planning and furnishings of some of the day nurseries. . . .

Yet the whole effort is not merely to make the world beautiful for the child. He is being given his own chances for creating beauty for himself. The teaching of the craft is fast creeping into the schools with more and more success.

Rho Fisk Zueblin, "The Arts and Crafts Movement: The Education of the Producer and the Consumer," The Chautauquan, *May 1903*

Chapter Six

The Society of Arts and Crafts, Boston

THIS SOCIETY WAS INCORPORATED FOR THE PURPOSE OF PROMOTING ARTISTIC WORK IN branches of handicraft. It hopes to bring Designers and Workmen into mutually helpful relations, and to encourage workmen to execute designs of their own. It endeavors to stimulate in workmen an appreciation of the dignity and value of good design; to counteract the popular impatience of Law and Form, and the desire for over-ornamentation and specious originality. It will insist upon the necessity of sobriety and restraint, of ordered arrangement, of due regard for the relation between the form of an object and its use, and of harmony and fitness in the decoration put upon it.

Established in 1897, the Society of Arts and Crafts, Boston, was comprised of architects and craftsworkers. Not only setting aesthetic and ethical standards, it promoted members' work by exhibitions, sales, and by the publishing of Handicraft *Magazine.*

Herbert Broadfield Warren, secretary, revised prospectus pamphlet of The Society of Arts and Crafts, Boston, Massachusetts, fall 1898

Guilds & Communities

Principles of Handicrafts

I. MOTIVES. The motives of the true Craftsman are the love of good and beautiful work as applied to useful service, and the need of making an adequate livelihood. In no case can it be primarily the love of gain.

II. CONDITIONS. The conditions of true Handicraft are natural aptitude, thorough technical training, and a just appreciation of standards. The unit of labor should be an intelligent man, whose ability is used as a whole, and not subdivided for commercial purposes. He should exercise the faculty of design in connection with manual work, and manual work should be part of his training in design.

III. ARTISTIC CO-OPERATION. When the designer and the workman are not united in the same person, they should work together, each teaching the other his own special knowledge, so that the faculties of the designer and the workman may tend to become united in each.

IV. SOCIAL CO-OPERATION. Modern Craftsmanship requires that the idea of patronage be superseded by that of reciprocal service and co-operation.

V. RESULTS. The results aimed at are the training of true craftsmen, the developing of individual character in connection with artistic work, and the raising of standards of beauty in objects of use.

"It is only possible to answer for the final truth of principles, not for the direct success of plans."

As published in the magazine Handicraft, *issued by the Society of Arts & Crafts, Boston*

Gild of Arts and Crafts of New York

HE AIM OF THE GILD, as set forth in its constitution, is to advance the union of the Arts of Design with the Arts of Production; with the ideal that the artist and artisan should be one and the same person. It is also purposed to establish shops which shall take the form of permanent exhibition, and sales rooms, where the work of the gild members and pupils, after passing a jury, shall be placed, also to co-operate actively with any organization interested in the progress of education and industry.

"Exhibition of the Gild of Arts & Crafts of New York," The Craftsman, *May 1902*

The Rochester Arts and Crafts Society

T IS THE PURPOSE of the Rochester Arts and Crafts Society to stimulate endeavor, not only in every branch of the arts proper, but in the application of art to industry; to encourage individual work in the making beautiful of all kinds of common and necessary manufactured articles, and to familiarize the lay public with the various processes through which such articles and works of art must pass in their making.

A Collection of Japanese Prints and Modern French Posters, *The Rochester Arts & Crafts Society, exhibition catalog Rochester, New York, 1897*

Guilds & Communities

 A HOME MUST BE CONSIDERED NOT ONLY FROM the personal standpoint, but also in relation to the community; and since a house once built must stand for many years, much thought should be given to the building to make it one that will add to the beauty of the neighbourhood.

Mable Tuke Priestman, Artistic Homes, *1910*

More than any other form of housing, the so-called California bungalow embodied the democratic spirit of the era. They were often made by nonprofessionals working from plan books; they were available through mail-order catalogs; they were homey and picturesque—thus popular. The rows of bungalows, which were built up during the first two decades of this century, represent the turn-of-the- century vision of the good life, a family-oriented life, and a sense of community.

53

Village Industries at Deerfield

The organization of village industries is one of the most important aspects of the young arts and crafts movement that is taking root in many parts of the land. Although the movement is so new, it gives evidence of a most genuine and wholesome growth in the way in which it is establishing itself here and there—not as an exotic that needs assiduous culture to keep it at its best, but as something that invites the expression, in free and natural ways, of tendencies and capacities, which need only the stimulus of intelligent encouragement to enable them to flourish and bear fruit. In various communities most interesting examples of these tendencies are already seen at work. Most notable is the development

of the movement in the historic and beautiful old Connecticut-Valley town of Deerfield in Massachusetts, where, in diverse ways, this and that branch of handicraft has established itself and become a part of the community life. All have thus come together as individual features of an organized whole that furnishes the instrumentality whereby each and all, through each and all, are enabled to make the best of themselves.

Sylvester Baxter, "The Movement for Village Industries," Handicraft, *October 1902*

Guilds & Communities

A Crafts Community at Rose Valley

Strong in their faith, men, women and children to the number of sixty or more have made their homes at Rose Valley. Here they have established a furniture shop in which no work is done that will not bear the most severe scrutiny as to honesty and thoroughness of construction; no sham, no pretense to do something outside of its evident use, will pass for good work. Here a metal working shop is being set up. Here the weaver, the potter, the printer and whatever other craftsman you will may have his shop. . . . Here are slowly gathering together people who do things —writers, musicians, craftsmen, art workers, and those who think a simple life with some human touch worth more than the strain and show and haphazard of your ordinary communities.

The Artsman, October 1903

A drawing of Rose Valley by Will Price as published in The Artsman

Arts and Crafts Ideals

WE DO NOT need to be reminded that the dream of the world for ages has been the ideal city of the future—a community which will unite with the fullest civic life and opportunity, the freedom and healthfulness of the country, and in which the citizens, merely because of their citizenship, will be entitled to share in all the benefits of the commonwealth. In this ideal community . . . the very failings of human nature—the self-seeking and combativeness which are the life blood of individualism—will be transmuted by the new conditions of life into recognition of, and striving for, the wider good which includes the whole community; class antagonism will be replaced by mutual understanding and good will, and all alike will have the op-

The Garden City

portunity to live, work and enjoy. . . .

The chief object of the promoters of the garden city idea has been to bring about a spontaneous movement of the people back to the land by creating conditions that will give them the advantages of city and country life combined, and to keep the whole thing on an economic basis that will afford comfort and prosperity to people of very moderate means. 🍂🍂🍂

The Editor, "Rapid Growth of the Garden City Movement Which Promises to Re-Organize Social Conditions All Over the World," The Craftsman, *November 1909. Originating in England with the innovative designs of Barry Parker and Raymond Unwin, the Garden City movement was inspired by Ebenezer Howard's* Tomorrow: A Peaceful Path to Real Reform *(1898), which suggested a new type of a semi-rural community.*

Guilds & Communities

WHEN AT LAST WE build the house of the democrat, its doors shall be wide and unbarred, for why should men steal who are free to make. It shall be set in a place of greenery, for the world is a large place and its loveliness mostly a wilderness; it shall be far enough away from its next for privacy and not too far for neighborliness; it shall have a little space knit within a garden wall; flowers shall creep up to its warmth, and flow, guided, but unrebuked over wall and low-drooped eaves. The rooms of his house shall be ample, and low, wide-windowed, deep-seated, spacious, cool by reason of shadows in summer, warm by the ruddy

The House of the Democrat

glow of firesides in winter, open to wistful summer airs, tight closed against the wintry blasts: a house, a home, a shrine; a little democracy unjealous of the greater world, and pouring forth the spirit of its own sure justness for the commonwealth. 🍂🍂🍂

Will Price, "The House of the Democrat," The Craftsman, *1911*

A bungalow from Henry Wilson's A Short Sketch of the Evolution of the Bungalow, *1909*

Chapter Seven

Why, in a democratic institution, do we speak of laboring (slave), middle (commercial), and the wealthy (the privileged) classes? Where classes are constantly mingling and exchanging positions this system has no meaning. Why not divide humanity once and for all into the slothful, the industrious and the constructive. In this way we could, at least, start in a venture for a better system of recompenses and penalties that *Society* has devised so far. Perhaps in the ultimate of things it might be uncoverd that a legitimate recompense for a day's work is based on the necessities of the life of the average individual balanced with his ability, in a given environment, to meet requirements.

Arthur and Lucia Mathews created furniture, stained glass, frames, paintings, books, and the magazine Philopolis *at* The Furniture Shop *(1906–1920) in San Francisco, California.*

Decorations on this page are designed by Lucia Mathews and were used in Philopolis, *August 1909*

The Reform of Society

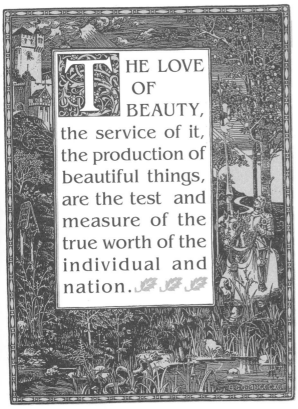

THE LOVE OF BEAUTY, the service of it, the production of beautiful things, are the test and measure of the true worth of the individual and nation.

From the first issue of
THE·KNIGHT·ERRANT

Printed by Boston's Elzevir Press and edited by Bertram Grosvenor Goodhue and Ralph Adams Cram, The Knight Errant (1892–93) had support from men like Charles Eliot Norton, Fred Holland Day, Ernest Fenollosa and Arthur Wesley Dow. As the cover design by Goodhue demonstrated, the knights tried to "war against the Paynims of realism in art, to assail the dragon of materialism, and the fierce dragon of mammonism, to ride for the succour of forlorn hopes and the restoration of forgotten ideals."

59

The Maker's Pleasure

WHEN THE consumer finds in the goods he has purchased no appeal to memory or associations, no real adjustment between the body and its garments, he can experience no genuine pleasure or rational satisfaction—in most cases the shoes actually pinch his feet, and the clothes constrain some part of the body. The fault is not with the materials, or with the form—considered abstractly—are not in workmanship or the style; still there is no pleasure to the user. Unless goods that are costly, perfect in their workmanship, tasteful in their design, serve an individual need, they are inappropriate, and in reality ugly and painful. If on the other hand the article evidences the maker's pleasure, his affection for his work, his play of memory and intelligence and faith, or if it is constructed with reference to another's need, and represents some claim of the soul for outer garment; if, in fine, the work be individualized, it becomes to that degree a work of art, a part of men's lives, the source of happiness.

Oscar Lovell Triggs, Chapters in the History of the Arts & Crafts Movement, *1902*

A Univesity of Chicago professor, Triggs was the organizer of the Industrial Art League, which lasted from 1899 to 1905. It advocated that, in an ideal economy, the crafts workshop should replace the factory and instead of working in manufacturing, workers should be participating in all facets of production.

The Reform of Society

LL THROUGH the ages kings and wealth have been patrons and eager purchasers of art crafts, not only of former times but of contemporary artists. It remained for young America, who has been too busy just growing, to neglect contemporary and native arts and crafts so that no country is so lacking in native craftsmen and crafts work. When, by chance, a craftsman does arrive, he has a hard struggle for recognition. Those who have acquired money, not having as a rule, acquired culture along with it. Patriotic and cultured men from time to time have given to museums, collections of art crafts of the past ages, in the dim hope that American talent might be inspired to follow the good examples. But they have failed to see that contemporary talent has to be encouraged by purchase of the best in native work.

Adlaide Alsop Robineau, letter to Fernando Carter, November 12, 1915

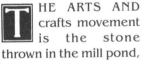

HE ARTS AND crafts movement is the stone thrown in the mill pond, small in itself yet causing waves that spread to the uttermost parts of the pond. The movement instills into the working man a desire for artistic labor, that expresses his own individuality, and it prompts the public to look to the artistic in making their purchases. It is the leaven which keeps alive the artistic sense.

Charles Rohlfs, The Chautauqua Assembly Herald, July 15, 1902

An Assessment

WHILE THE ARTICLES produced by handicraft in the United States are of small value compared with the products of machinery, and cannot be expected to increase to such an extent as to diminish noticeably the demand for factory products, the revival of handicrafts is of no little importance to a considerable number of persons. The workers themselves are perhaps the persons most affected, and in many cases the Arts and Crafts movement has brought to them at once a means of livelihood and a new interest in life.

> **T**HE Love you Liberate in your Work is the only Love you Keep—*Fra Elbertus*

To the consumers, and the public generally, the movement has brought increased pleasure in the things of daily household use and ornament. The artistic and industrial importance of the handicraft revival cannot be measured by the quantity of handmade goods produced, for the standards of durability and taste set by the craftsmen make their influence felt in improving the quality and design of factory-made goods; and this, however far it may be from the intention of the craftsmen, is perhaps the most far-reaching effect of their work.

Max West, "The Revival of Handicrafts in America," Bulletin of the Bureau of Labor, No. 55, November 1904

Index

Arts & Crafts Ideals was composed with the fonts Benguiat for text and Benguiat and Gorilla for titles and was designed using or adapting period graphics from the turn-of-the-century. Sources are as follows unless already noted in the body of the book.

The cover and title page border and decoration are adopted from designs by Dard Hunter for *White Hyacinths,* Roycroft, 1907. ✤ P. 5 decoration from *Chicago Tongue,* Roycroft, 1900. ✤ P. 7 initial capital (hereafter I.C.) from *The Graphic Arts: for Printers and Users of Printing,* January 1911. ✤ P. 10 border and P. 11 I.C. from *Love, Life & Work,* Roycroft, 1906. ✤ P. 11 logo for Rose Valley from *The Artsman,* 1906. ✤ P. 12 I.C. from *Composition,* 1899. ✤ P. 14 advertisement for The Grueby Pottery from collection of The Arts & Crafts Press. ✤ P. 17 logo for Charles Rohlfs courtesy of Robert Judson Clark. ✤ P. 18 vase decoration is by Margaret Overbeck from *Keramic Studio,* June 1906. ✤ P. 21 design based on Maybeck's design for the First Church of Christ, Scientist, Berkeley, 1910.

P. 23 illustration is adapted from a page of *Composition,* 1899. ✤ P. 24 drawing from *Woodwork for Secondary Schools,* 1916. The I.C. was designed by Yoshiko Yamamoto. ✤ P. 25 drawing from *Pallete and Bench,* September 1910. ✤ P. 26 border from *Our Telephone Service,* Roycroft, 1913. ✤ P. 27 I.C. from *Love, Life & Work,* Roycroft, 1906. ✤ P. 28 I.C. from *The Roycroft Books: A Catalog and Some Remarks,* 1902. ✤ P. 29 decoration adopted from a design by Louis Sullivan for his 1889 Auditorium Building. ✤ P. 30 leftside tree P. 31 tree and I.C. from *Nature,* Roycroft, 1905. ✤ P. 30 border and decorations from *A Catalogue of Some Books made by the Roycrofters,* 1907. ✤ P. 34-35 border and decorations from *Justinian and Theodora,* Roycroft, 1906. ✤ P. 38 drawing from *The Craftsman,* May 1916. ✤ P. 41 portrait of Charles Wagner from an original advertisement for *The Simple Life,* 1901. ✤ P. 42 illustrations are from *The School Arts Magazine,* leftside from September, 1920; rightside from September, 1911. ✤ P. 43 adapted from *The Graphic Arts,* 1911. ✤

P. 45 based on Maybeck's desig[n] for the First Church of Chris[t,] Scientist, Berkeley, 1910. ✤ [P.] 46 I.C. and plate from *Th[e] Craftsman* magazine. ✤ P. 4[?] from *The Fra,* March 1913. ✤ P. 49 motto from *The Schoo[l] Arts* magazine, Septembe[r] 1911. I.C. from *Text Books o[f] Art Education: Book VI: Sixt[h] Year,* 1905. ✤ P. 50 catalo[g] cover from the First Exhibitio[n] of the Arts & Crafts catalo[g] cover, 1897. ✤ P. 52 I.C fro[m] *The Craftsman* ✤ P. 53 draw[?]ing from *The Craftsman* and th[e] I.C. from *Home Building an[d] Decoration,* 1912. ✤ P. 5[?] drawing adapted from [a] Deerfield needlework design. ✤ P. 59 border from *The Knight E[r]rant,* 1892, and the I.C. fro[m] *Sonnets from the Portugese* Copeland and Day, 1896—bot[h] designed by Bertrum Grosveno[r] Goodhue. ✤ P. 62 I.C. fro[m] *White Hyacinths,* Roycroft, 190[?] and the motto is from *The Mott[o] Book,* Roycroft, 1909. ✤ I.C. o[f] PP. 20, 21, 36, 37, 39, 40, 4[?] 45, 56, 57, 60, and 61 ar[e] *Oldstyle* from *American Typ[e] Founder's Specimen Book* 1904. ✤✤✤